Editors: Christian Hanus, Gerald Steiner
Book Design and Page Layout: Thomas Pfeffer, Richard Sickinger
Editing, Proof Reading: Porfiro Guevara, Florian Kerschbaumer,
Richard Sickinger, Heidemarie Weinhäupl
Cover Photo: Donau-Universität Krems/Archiv, www.fotolia.com

Edition Donau-Universität Krems

ISBN
Paperback   978-3-903150-31-7
e-Book   978-3-903150-38-6

Printed on demand in many countries. Distributed by tredition
Krems, January 2019, 1st Edition

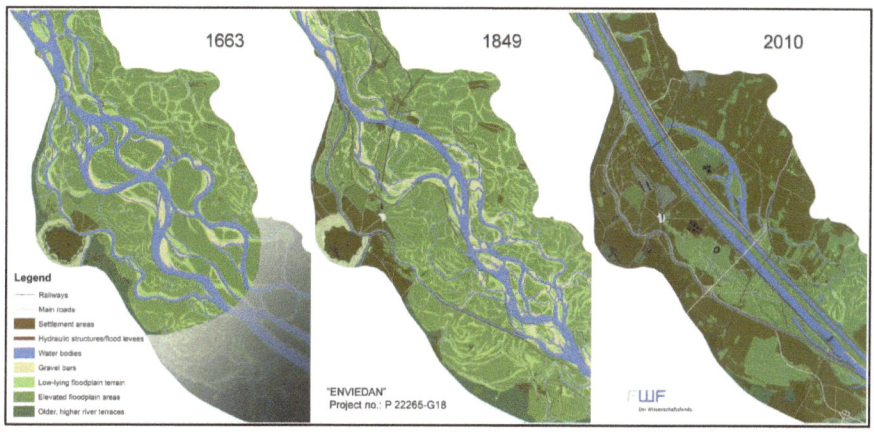

Legend	
Railways	
Main roads	
Settlement areas	
Hydraulic structures/flood levees	
Water bodies	
Gravel bars	
Low-lying floodplain terrain	
Elevated floodplain areas	
Older, higher river terraces	

1663   1849   2010

"ENVIEDAN"
Project no.: P 22265-G18

FWF
Der Wissenschaftsfonds.

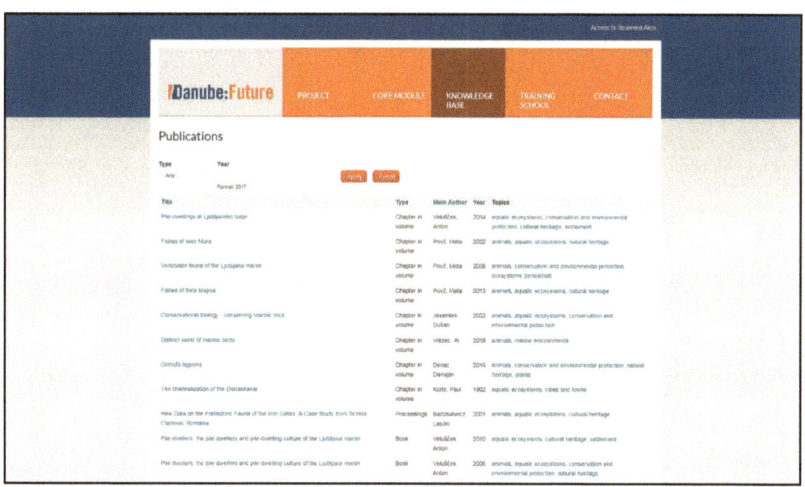

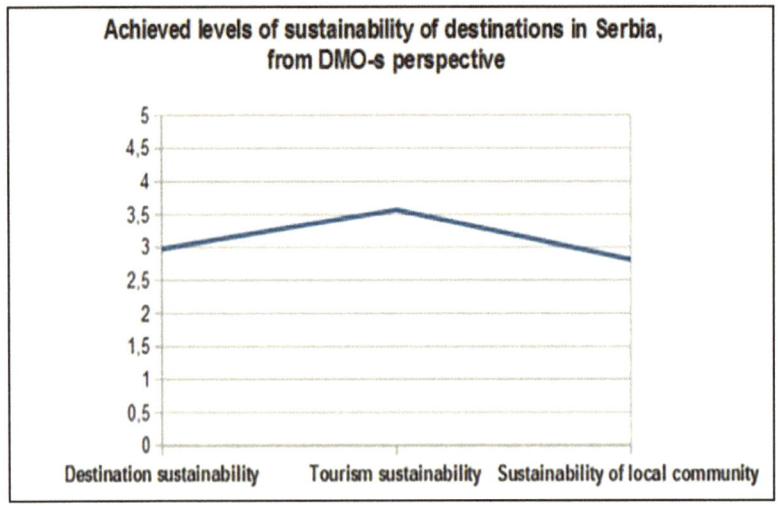

Achieved levels of sustainability of destinations in Serbia, from DMO-s perspective

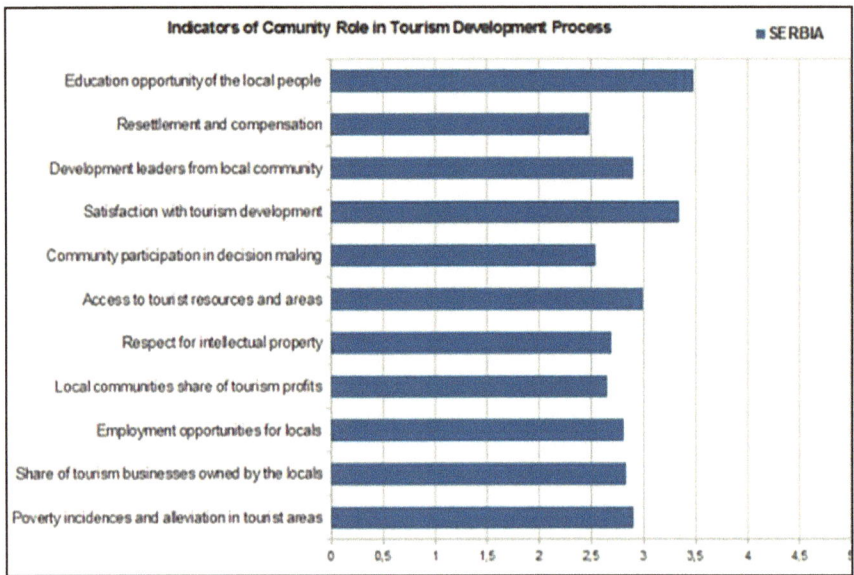

Indicators of Comunity Role in Tourism Development Process

The assessment of the feasibility of the study has been done in 5 aspects to evaluate the project's potential for success. 1) Technical feasibility - assessment is centred on the technical resources available for the organization. Technical and scientific aspects have been evaluated and described in WPs 2-7; 2) Economic feasibility - costs associated with projects estimated for financial resources allocation; 3) Legal feasibility - investigations have been done to verify if the proposed system conflicts with legal requirements. 4) Operational feasibility - a study has been done to determine whether the functional needs can be fulfilled. Hiring a subcontractor is suggested after first cycle of planting; 5) Schedule feasibility is the most important for project success. This study has been done for one cycle of planting.

According to Figure 2, the critical path of the Gantt chart will need 5 years to be accomplished. The schedule was made for one cycle of phytoremediation and the next strategies will be planned according to the results of the first cycle. Time schedule is based on the example of phytoremediation by sunflower within the period of 1.5 year (the selection of the specific plants will be based on the results from the WP3 in the first step of WP4).

Figure 2. PlantPower project timeline with defined work packages (WPs).

WP2 - Localization of mine sites for phytoremediation process in Croatia and Bosnia and Herzegovina

The objective of WP2 is to create a detailed database, based on the already available information from HRC and BHMAC (sources: https://www.hcr.hr and http://www.bhmac.org), on the temporal and special distribution of former minefields in the Danube River Basin of the Western Balkan Area, particularly on the Sava/Danube stretch in Croatia and BiH that are appropriate for future phytoremediation. Minefields suitable for phytoremediation will be chosen according to the possibility of their usage for agricultural purposes. Data regarding cleaned minefields will be regularly updated by the participating project partners.

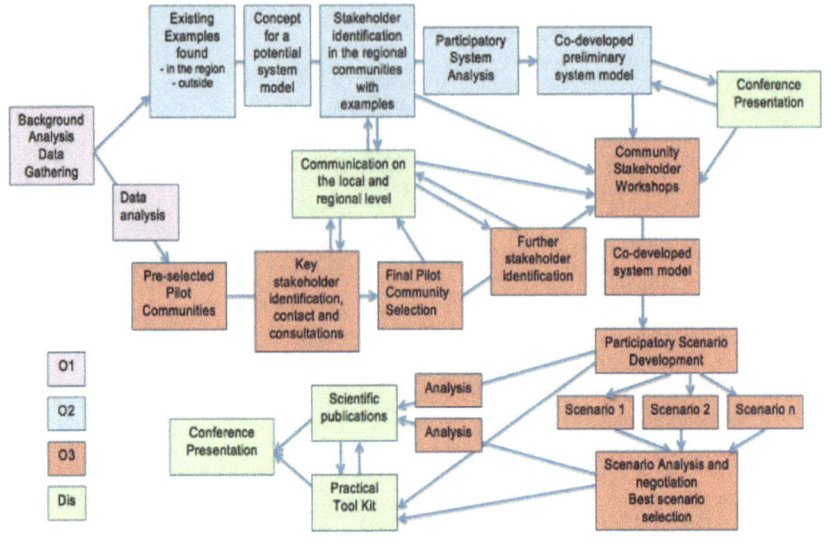

WP	Task	Iron Gate - the Green Re-Opening																																				P1	P2	P3	P4	P5	P6
		1	2	3	4	5	6	7	8	9	10	11	12	13	14	15	16	17	18	19	20	21	22	23	24	25	26	27	28	29	30	31	32	33	34	35	36						
WP 1.Management (coordination, project partner meetings, quality control, reporting) (University of Natural Resources and Life Sciences, Vienna (BOKU), AT)	Kick-off meeting of the project team																																					x	x	x	x	x	x
	project management and coordination																																					x					
	6 team-meetings per 6 months																																					x					
WP 2. Background research, data gathering and analysis (University of Constanta, RO)	Background analysis gathering by each country team via interdisciplinary approach																																					x	x	x	x	x	x
	Analysing data																																					x	x	x	x	x	x
	Discussing and finalising the analytical review, based on the interdisciplinary conclusions																																					x	x				
WP 3. Identification and system analysis of existing examples (Serbian Academy of Sciences and Arts, Geographical Institute "Jovan Cvijić", SRB)	Finding out existing examples of revived small communities																																					x	x	x	x	x	x
	Discussing and creating a preliminary system model to revitalising the comunities through economic initiatives																																					x	x	x	x	x	x
	Identifying the involved stakeholders to peticipate in locally - based forum sessions for discussions																																					x	x	x	x	x	x
	Negotiating the model together with the local communities																																					x	x	x	x	x	x
WP 4. Stakeholder involvement and pilot testing (Ruse University, BG)	Seeding pilot communities to test the preliminary model																																					x	x	x	x	x	x
	Identifying stakeholders and local partners in the selected communities and organising workshops																																					x	x	x	x	x	x
	Performing local workshops to discuss the possible implementation of the preliminary model																																					x	x	x	x	x	x
	Final workshops with the stakeholders to perform best scenario selection																																					x	x	x	x	x	x
	Organising 5 public conferences for dissemination																																					x	x	x	x	x	x
WP 5. Dissemination (REC, HU)	Participating in 2 scientific conferences for dissemination																																					x	x	x	x	x	x
	Organising and performing press conferences																																					x	x	x	x	x	x
	Setting up and maintaining e-communication through social media, web page and newsletter																																					x	x	x	x	x	x
WP	Task	1	2	3	4	5	6	7	8	9	10	11	12	13	14	15	16	17	18	19	20	21	22	23	24	25	26	27	28	29	30	31	32	33	34	35	36	P1	P2	P3	P4	P5	P6

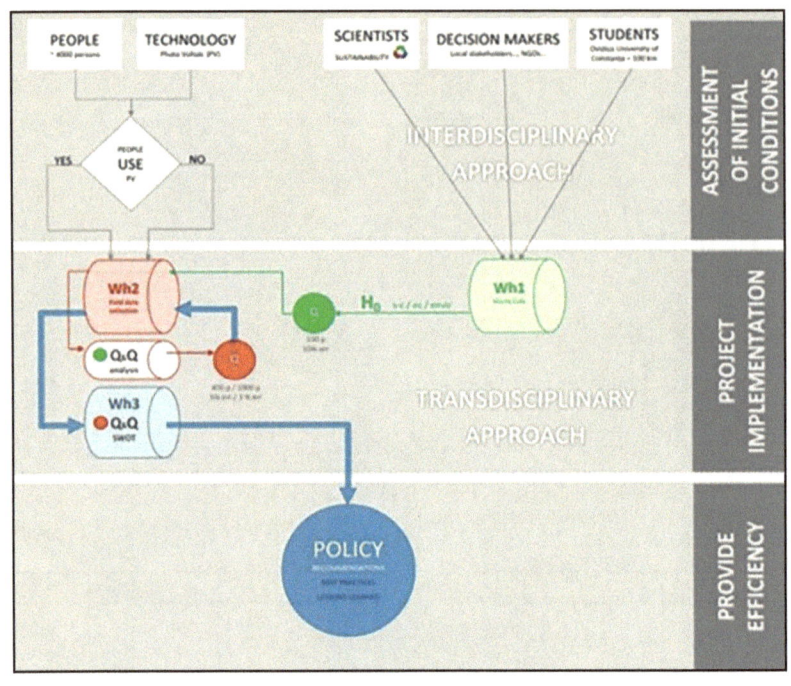

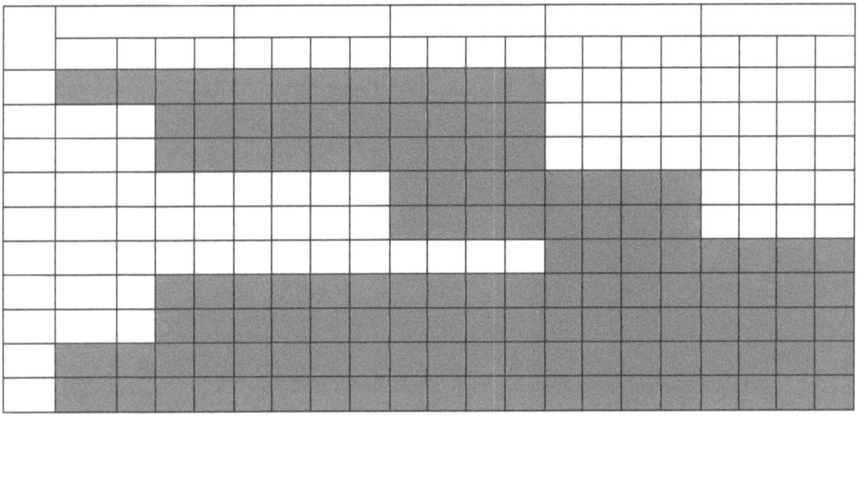

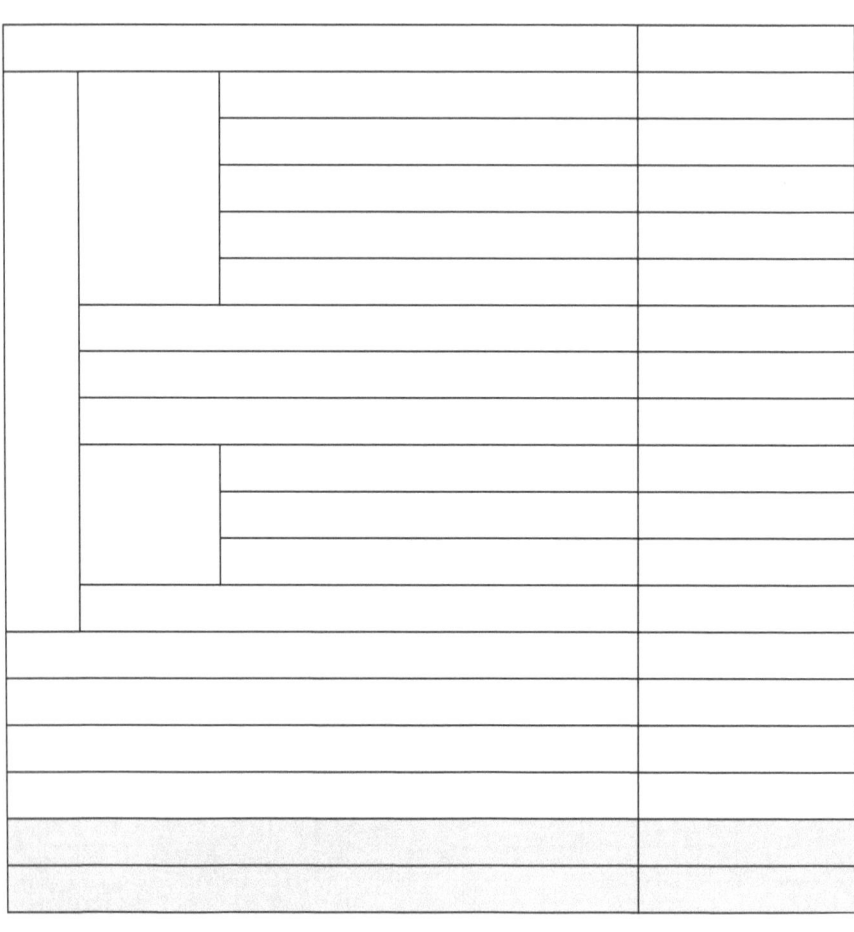

Zeitfracht Medien GmbH
Ferdinand-Jühlke-Straße 7
99095 Erfurt, Deutschland
produktsicherheit@kolibri360.de